THE WAR BOYS

Naomi Wallace

BROADWAY PLAY PUBLISHING INC
56 E 81st St., NY NY 10028-0202
212 772-8334 fax: 212 772-8358
http://www.BroadwayPlayPubl.com

THE WARBOYS
© Copyright 1997 by Naomi Wallace

First printing: November 2004
I S B N: 0-88145-253-X

Book design: Marie Donovan
Word processing: Microsoft Word
Typographic controls: Xerox Ventura Publisher 2.0 P E
Typeface: Palatino
Printed and bound in the U S A

ABOUT THE AUTHOR

Naomi Wallace is from Kentucky. Her play TRESTLE
AT POPE LICK CREEK, was produced at Actor's
Theater of Louisville in 1998, then New York Theater
Workshop in 1999, and the Travers Theater of
Edinburgh, Scotland and the Southwark Theater of
London in 2002 and 2003 respectively. THE INLAND
SEA premiered in London in 2002, produced by the
Oxford Stage Company. Her short play, THE
RETREATING WORLD, has been produced in London,
Amsterdam, Germany and France.

Her play ONE FLEA SPARE was commissioned and
produced in October 1995 by the Bush Theatre in
London. It received its American premiere at the
Humana Festival and was awarded the 1996 Susan
Smith Blackburn Prize, the 1996 Fellowship of Southern
Writers Drama Award, the 1996 Kesselring Prize, and
the 1997 Obie Award for best play.

SLAUGHTER CITY was awarded the 1995 Mobil Prize
and received its world premiere in January 1996 at the
Royal Shakespeare Company. IN THE HEART OF
AMERICA received its world premiere at the Bush
Theatre in London and subsequently was produced
at The Long Wharf Theater. It was awarded the 1995
Susan Smith Blackburn Prize. Her plays are published
in Great Britain by Faber and Faber.

Wallace was a 1999 recipient of the prestigious MacArthur Fellowship, the grant popularly known as the "genius" award.

A published poet in both England and in The United States, she received a 1997 N E A grant for poetry. Her book of poetry, *To Dance A Stony Field*, was published in the United Kingdom.

Her film *Lawn Dogs*, produced by Duncan Kenworthy, has won numerous film awards.

At present, Wallace is under commission by the Guthrie Theater, and National Theater of Britain. With her partner, Bruce McLeod, she is adapting Michael Ondaatje's *In the Skin of a Lion* for Serendipity Films, and *The Golden Warrior* (on the battle of Hastings) for Young Films.

ORIGINAL PRODUCTION

THE WAR BOYS had its first performance on 10 February 1993 at the Finborough Theater. The cast and creative contributors were:

Bradley Lavelle
Mathew Sharp
Ethan Flower

Director . . . . .Kate Valentine
Design . . . . Fay Saxty
Music . . . . .Alex Valentine

CHARACTERS & SETTING

GREG, *early twenties, Mexican-American, working class*
DAVID, *early twenties, college educated, privileged*
GEORGE, *early twenties, "home boy"*

Time: Now

Place: At a place that could be the Mexico/Texas border

(The set is minimal and by no means "realistic". A part of a barbed wire fence, to suggest a "border", is visible. The three men enter the stage one at a time. Each one is carrying a heavy-duty spotlight. With a look of mutual consent they take up their positions. They're now going to "play" the War Boys game. They play this game for real. The three of them crouch on a raised area of the stage in silence, scanning the border, until DAVID points at something he sees moving out there.)

DAVID: Put the brights on. Now! Now!

(They turn their spotlights on toward the public.)

GEORGE: Fuckin' beaner. Look at him run!

DAVID: Sweet Christ, he's wearing my Adidas.

GEORGE: Call him down, Greg. He's slipping away.

GREG: This is car six of the War Boys. We got a slowrider sighted making for the crossing at fence line nine.

GEORGE: *(Grabs mike from GREG)* Should we go after him? Over. *(Listens)* Says he'll send a car over after he makes a stop at the ditch line.

DAVID: Dim them again.

(Lights are dimmed)

DAVID: I think we lost him. When he starts up the hill. Oh yes, yes, look at him sprint.

GEORGE: Ninja, ninja, ninja.

DAVID: Think I wasted four years at Stanford for nothing?

GREG: Shit. Shit. He's in reverse.

DAVID: Come back, Marlboro Man. Come back to the Marlboro Land!

GEORGE: Damn. We lost him.

GREG: He'll be back.

DAVID: *(To GREG)* How come you were late tonight? I like to start on time.

GREG: Sorry. Had to finish up at the library.

DAVID: Oh? Beating off on Chaucer again, hey, Greggie.

GEORGE: Who's she?

DAVID: The Wife of Bath, yeah, baby.

GEORGE: *(Hears something)* Hey, did you hear that?

GREG: Sure. Swabbin' floors I get a lot of time to read. *(Beat)* I saw the other guys. They're at five tonight.

DAVID: Well, we're stuck right here until ten, then line seventeen 'til midnight.

GEORGE: Hey, want to see a trick?

GREG: By the way, David, it's a known fact that rich boys beat off three point seven times more than poor boys. Know why? *(Holds up his hands to DAVID's face)*

GEORGE: I can hold a cigarette with my dick.

GREG: Because guys like me haven't got, excuse me, I mean "ain't" got all that free, leisure, wack-wack time.

GEORGE: Can we make it an early night tonight? Little bro is sick again.

DAVID: He's always sick. Take the kid to the doctor for a change why don't you.

GEORGE: Nothing I can't cure.

DAVID: With T L C, huh, Georgia?

GEORGE: Why not? Think I haven't got it in me?

DAVID: *(Sniffs)* Smell that aroma? It's the feminine scent. I'm going to pick up its trail.

(DAVID snorts, then throws himself to the ground and begins to belly-crawl about the stage, searching for something across the "border". GEORGE and GREG ignore him.)

GEORGE: It's your go.

GREG: I'm not in the mood.

GEORGE: It's your go.

GREG: No thanks.

GEORGE: Come on. You promised. You played it with David last time.

(GEORGE rolls up his sleeve and after some moments, GREG does so wearily. Then GREG slaps GEORGE, though not hard, across the face. As they converse. GEORGE returns the slap, somewhat harder. Each slaps the other harder until one of them loses their balance. Meanwhile, DAVID is still crawling about sniffing.)

GREG: So who's our contact tonight?

(Slaps GEORGE)

GEORGE: Officer Sharons.

GREG: Shit. Sharons is a drunk ass. Always too slow on the call-up.

GEORGE: *(Slaps GREG)* He says there's a hole they're getting through somewhere from three through seven.

GREG: *(Slaps GEORGE)* There's always a hole.

GEORGE: You ever notice something funny about my smile, Greg? *(Slaps GREG)*

GREG: Ask me about your breath.

GEORGE: *(Slaps GEORGE)* No, boy. The smile.

(Grins hugely and holds it. GREG slaps him hard.)

GREG: Food. In the corner of your mouth.
(Slaps GEORGE) Hear that? Listen.

GEORGE: What?

GREG: Listen.

GEORGE: I don't hear anything. *(Beat)* For a mop-boy you sure are stupid.

(Slaps him hard. GREG is knocked off his seat.)

GEORGE: It never lasts more than ten hits with you. You're a wimp.

DAVID: *(Still crawling about)* Psst. Here sissy, sissy, sissy.

GEORGE: I mean it. What kind of animal do I smile like?

GREG: A worm. How about a worm?

GEORGE: Hey, David, what was that fancy-ass word for chewing you used the other night?

DAVID: I see you. I see you.

GREG: Masticate.

GEORGE: Yeah. What animal do I masticate like?
(Chews loudly)

DAVID: *(Whispers)* Come here. I won't hurt you.

GREG: A groundhog?

GEORGE: It's dead zone here.

(DAVID circles back to their area, grabs GREG's leg and clings to him, exaggerating.)

DAVID: Oh, Father, who art in heaven, help me to step down from this stifling perch. Help me to respect manual labor, so I can wear filthy overalls, so I can make money with my own bare hands and get out of those oppressive neighborhood recycling programs.

GEORGE: Let's move.

GREG: We've got to wait 'til ten.

(Shakes DAVID *off)*

GREG: Sorry, Buddy. Once an M C-er, always and M C-er.

GEORGE: What's an M C-er?

DAVID: Moose-Cuticle, you idiot.

GREG: Short for Middle Class.

DAVID: Go easy on him, Greg. He can only take a bit of learning at a time.

GEORGE: *(Baring his rear to* DAVID*)* Have a bite from my left cheek, Mr Diploma. *(Beat)* Hey, I've got a game we can play.

DAVID: *(Standing and composing himself. To* GEORGE:*)* Nope. We're going to play mine. *(To* GREG*)* I would like to bet you five dollars you can't, excuse my coarseness, jerk off while I'm saying the Pledge of Allegiance.

GEORGE: I bet I could.

DAVID: *(Still to* GREG*)* Five bucks you can't.

*(*GREG *ignores him.)*

GEORGE: *(Moves a good distance from them)* I'll do it over here.

DAVID: *(To* GEORGE*)* Nope, I'll need to see the evidence.

GREG: You two are kindergarten.

GEORGE: *(Moves closer)* O K, but no peeking.

DAVID: On your marks.

GREG: This is the last time I'm out with you two.

DAVID: Get set.

GREG: I just want to make that clear.

GEORGE: Go.

DAVID: I pledge allegiance to the flag, to the United States of America— *(He mimics a quarterback while he recites, both fast and slow.)* —and to the Republic for which it stands, one nation, under God, indivisible, with liberty and justice for all.

GEORGE: Start over.

DAVID: Five bucks. Now.

GEORGE: Fuck off. I already owe you two hundred and thirty.

DAVID: Now you owe me two hundred and thirty-five.

GEORGE: Yeah, well, I almost had you, bud. But when you got to the "and to the Republic" bit that brought me down.

DAVID: Your credit with me is going to drop, sir, if you can't improve your performance.

GREG: You two. Shit. *(Beat)* Listen, we stay in the car tonight or I'm quits with you guys.

GEORGE: *(To GREG)* Will you quit worrying?

GREG: I mean it.

GEORGE: We're friends, Greg. A promise is a promise.

DAVID: What about last Friday night? Standing on the sidelines observing it all. I could see it was tickling your palate.

GREG: *(Interrupts)* I was fucked up that night. I'm not like you dogs.

(DAVID meows.)

DAVID: But I polished my hood tonight especially.

GREG: Tonight we stay in the car and let the officers handle the rest.

DAVID: *(Pushing* GREG *with his finger)* Since when do you call the shots for this brigade? Hey? Who gives you a ride here in the evenings?

GREG: You do.

DAVID: Who pays for the gas?

GREG: You do.

DAVID: Who buys you your six-pack?

GREG: I just don't want things to get messy tonight.

GEORGE: Don't spoil the evening, Greg.

DAVID: Hey. I never swore I wasn't a sick individual now did I?

GEORGE: We'll be good. My bro's sick. I want to be home early. *(Gets on his knees and shouts towards the border, which is now the public)* Mama Mia. Come on, come on! Let's light this birthday cake!

DAVID: Hurry, hurry. Step right up. *(Kneels next to* GEORGE, *extends his arms to public)* See the greatest show on earth.

*(*GREG *now joins in. The tune for this song should give the sense of a chain-gang type ballad.)*

ALL: *(Border Song)*
On the border, we can see the pretty sights,
Some in the day, but the best ones at night
Bring a six-pack of Bud and a bag of chips
Bring some soda pop and some tamale dip.

We can spot them running, we can watch them crawl
We can tie them up, we can have a ball.
We can make ten dollars if we catch one alive
The Feds will pay us money and they'll give us no jive.

*(*DAVID *jumps up, toppling* GREG.)*

DAVID: Shhhh. Did you hear that?

GEORGE: What?

GREG: Where?

DAVID: Shhhhh. *(Sings again, but alone, as others tap out music)* Barbaric? A clear case of missing morality?
You're wrong, this fun's a duty from the highest
  authority
These beaners don't value life as we boys do
We heard it from the top, they want to mix a racial stew.

GREG: *(Sings)* Now we got dead-end jobs or the army
  option
We can travel to kill or we can sell the MacLuncheon.

GEORGE: *(Sings)* But why take orders or clean up
  someone's shit
When we can light up the border, ten dollars a hit.

DAVID: You know what I heard today? They say some
of our own kind have crossed over there.

(All three are on guard and nervous.)

GEORGE: Over there?

DAVID: Forming a so-called "protect the Mex" band.
(Beat) Could be they're carrying knives.

GREG: I don't think so.

DAVID: Could be they're carrying guns.

GEORGE: Guns?

GREG: Don't listen to him George.

DAVID: Scared, Greg?

GEORGE: Hey, I heard something.

DAVID: Shhhh. What was that?

GREG: George's gut.

DAVID: There it is again. Hear it?

(They all huddle.)

GEORGE: I heard it.

GREG: Shhhhh.

DAVID: Sounds like

GEORGE: Like

GREG: Like

DAVID: Like a knife sharpening on a stone.

GEORGE: *(Whispers)* Let's get out of here.

GREG: *(Whispers)* Just some stones rolling down the hill, George.

DAVID: *(Sees something)* What's that?

GEORGE: Where?

GREG: Where?

DAVID: Something shining. Two. Three things shining.

GEORGE: *(Whispers)* Let's go.

GREG: I don't see anything shining.

DAVID: *(Whispers)* Blades. Knife blades. *(Shouts)* Blades!

(As DAVID shouts he throws a knife in front of them, and GREG and GEORGE both scare and duck. Then DAVID is laughing at them.)

GEORGE: That's not very funny, David.

DAVID: With you two I can't resist.

GREG: *(Clutching his stomach)* Hold it.

DAVID: Must you repeat this performance every time there's a little excitment down here? I say "boo" and you puke.

(GREG moves upstage and begins to vomit.)

DAVID: Couldn't you get some pills to keep it down? You're pitiful, sweetheart.

GEORGE: *(Hands over ears)* That noise gets to me.

DAVID: Five bucks says I can make it worse for you, Greg.

(GREG is oblivious to them and continues being sick. GEORGE stands over him with his arm raised like the Statue of Liberty.)

DAVID: *(Sings)* America, America
God shed his grace on thee
And crown thy good
With brotherhood
From sea to shining sea

(As DAVID is still singing, GREG recovers and lights change slightly as he moves downstage right, near public, wiping his mouth on his sleeve.)

DAVID: You, my man, don't have the belly to take a joke.

GEORGE: Take it easy, Greg. He didn't see anything.

GREG: Yeah? Well, maybe I did.

(During GREG's monologue, GEORGE and DAVID carry on in and around the car area.They are not unaware of GREG's performance, rather they are not really interested in it. At times, however, they will intervene. GREG is addressing the border here.)

GREG: *(To border)* Hey! Hey! *Dame dos cuchillos.* Throw me a couple of knives. *(Turns back to his friends a moment)* Think I haven't got it in me? Maybe I'll just step over there and find out if they're carrying knives. *(Spits on his palms, smooths back his hair, addresses border again)* Think I haven't got it in me? Scared, are you? *(Beat)* Hey. I bet you never belonged to the Boy Scouts. I did. The church choir? *(Holds a note)* I could hold the longest note. Then I went on to join the Sunday Dixie Band. And then the Blueshell Campaign to save the farmers. Then I joined the Border Brigade. *(Lifts his shirt*

and draws an imaginary line down the center of his body)
This half of me is Mejicano. This other half of me is
WASP. *Como sabes* which side is which? My mother
was Mexican. She used to tell me: "*Este lado es Mejicano.*
This side is Mexican— *(Slaps left breast)* —the side with
the heart."

GEORGE: *(Spots something)* Look.

DAVID: Another one!

GEORGE: A beaner chick. In heat.

GREG: My father *me dijo* it was my lower half that was
WASP, that I had his *cojones*— *(Grabs crotch)* —but the
brains of a beaner. *(Beat)* When I was a little nino I was
two separate pieces, just below the surface, held
together by skin.

DAVID: Here she comes.

GEORGE: Throw the brights on her.

DAVID: Not yet, not yet. Wait.

GREG: Didn't do sports. Didn't run during recess.
Never got on a bike. *Nada ni mierda.* If I'd made the
wrong move I'd split, right down the center.

DAVID: You're missing the spectacle, Greggie.

GEORGE: Open the sun roof. Hey, baby. Slip under the
wire.

DAVID: We're the Holiday Inn.

GEORGE: The Light Up the Border Brigade.

GREG: *Mi padre*, he was a Senior *Agente* of the Border.
He used to take a lot of slack for having married a Wet.
But he always said it was strategy, that he knew them
better, inside and out, on account of her.

DAVID: Come and get your red, hot
one-hundred-percent American hard-on.

GEORGE: *(Sings)* It's the real thing...

GREG: They say he was a good cop.

DAVID: *(Sings)* That's the way it should be....

GREG: He made O K *dinero*, helped me get a loan
so I could get my first car. Then I met my first girl.
She was Chicana. *(Beat)* I figured, like father, like son.
And this *chica* was legal, nice trailer, two-parent family.
She wasn't real pretty, but she gave me a feeling *(Beat)*
like eatin' a bowl of frosted flakes with tequila. We
were planning on living together, so I brought her
home to meet my father.

DAVID: Look at that.

GEORGE: She's stuck.

DAVID: Her shirt's tangled up in the wire.

GREG: He called us into his office. I told him I was
thinking about marrying her. He took a hold of
Evalina's long braid and tipped her head back. *(Beat)*
Then he stuck his fingers in her mouth and tested her
molars. He found the hole where she'd just had a tooth
pulled. He jammed his nail in it, and she yelled. Then
he just shook his head. He was disappointed.

GEORGE: She can't get loose.

GREG: Then he took out his wallet. "You can't marry a
woman with a bad set of teeth," he said. "It spoils the
breath." He counted it out: *veinte, quarenta, sesenta, cien.*
Two hundred bucks.

DAVID: Come on, Godiva. A few more shakes, and I'll
let you polish the hood of my new mustang.

GREG: My Evalina was wearing an orange blouse that
day, with a blue ribbon braided into her hair.

DAVID: But she doesn't even look Mexican.

GEORGE: Maybe she's Arab.

GREG: He unbuttoned her blouse and tucked the money in her bra. *(Beat)* Then he kissed us both on the forehead.

DAVID: *(Shoving him)* Go on, George. Talk to her.

GEORGE: But I can't speak Spanish.

DAVID: Shit Spanish. She's a bitch. Give her poetry.

GREG: Over breakfast the next morning he asked me if I'd made the appointment with the dentist.

GEORGE: *Chica, chica.*

GREG: I said yes. I told him me and Evalina, we both appreciated his advice.

DAVID: Not that. Marvell, stupid. Watch this: "When as in silks my...beaner goes, then, then, methinks how sweetly flows the greasafaction of her clothes. Next when I cast mine..."

GEORGE: It worked. She's grinnin' like a raccoon. Hey, hamburguesa!

GREG: I suppose Evalina went and got her teeth fixed. I don't know. She wouldn't see me after that.

DAVID: This is America. Over ninety billion served.

GREG: I mean, *mi padre*, he was a strict man sometimes, but he looked out for me.

GEORGE: Move over. Let me out of the car.

GREG: *(To* GEORGE *and* DAVID, *who have begun to encroach too far on his story)* Stay in the fuckin' car, George.

GEORGE: The lady needs to be rescued. *(To* DAVID Just watch this. You watching?

GREG: Asshole. We've got a deal with the Feds. We spot them. That's all. If we fuck up again...

GEORGE: Fuck you, Greg. Hey, *muchacha*!!

DAVID: Look at old Georgie. He's combing back his hair.

GREG: You two baboon asses are fuckin' up my thing.

(Pushes GEORGE *back)*

GREG: Can't you shut up just a few more seconds until I'm done?

*(*GEORGE *and* DAVID *mock-freeze. For some seconds* GREG *doesn't know where to pick up again.)*

GREG: I suppose Evalina got her teeth fixed. I don't know. She wouldn't see me after that...

DAVID: *(Interrupts)* No, no. You left off at *(Mocks* GREG's *voice)* "He was a strict man, but he looked out for me."

GREG: Yeah. Thanks. *(Beat)* But he looked out for me. It was about a year later, and I came home to visit my mother. I told her about me and Evalina being over, about how Father had offered to pay to fix her teeth. I watched her pour a whole bottle of detergent into the washer. Then she said, like she might have been saying "hand me a towel", "And you let him do that?" *(Beat)* Then she smacked me across the face. Not hard. But it was the first time she ever hit me. Then she just kept saying it, over and over: *"Y lo dejaste hacerlo?" And you let him do that?*

DAVID: *(Louder)* And you let him do that?

GEORGE: *(Louder)* And you let him do that?

GREG: I almost said, "She was just a fuckin' beaner, Ma." *(Begins to laugh)* Wouldn't have been the appropriate thing to say. When my father walked through the door that night, "bang", she hit him over the head with a dinner plate. *(Raises arms slowly as though holding a gun and fires)* Bang...bang...bang... A few years later, my father *se murio*. Dead. I dragged around the half of me *que fue muerte*, his dead half. Sometimes I'd wake up in the middle of the night and I'd smell its deadness, like rotten cantaloupe. *(Beat)* So that's why I joined up. Because, even though my mother died shortly after, the beaner half of me wouldn't die.

DAVID: Hold it!

(He hurries over and lifts up GREG's *foot.)*

Look at this. You're standing on a sapling. How many times do I have to tell you to watch where the hell you're standing. Lucky you didn't break the poor little fellow's back. Go stand somewhere else.

*(*GREG *moves a few feet away.)*

GREG: Here?

*(*DAVID *motions with his hand for* GREG *to move a little farther.)*

GREG: Here?

*(*DAVID *nods O K and returns to the car.* GREG *continues)*

GREG: As a matter of fact, the beaner half of me began to move in on the other half. In no time at all I was seventy-percent beaner, and it keeps spreading. Before I know it, *uno, dos, tres,* I'll be a hundred-percent pure beef wetback. I'm feeling it in my bones. And my feet, they want to dance that cockroach song. *(Does a mild tapdance of sorts)* But every time we catch one of those Mejicanos crossing the border, the pressure eases up. *Y puedo descansar.*

DAVID: Look, George. She's still there. Waiting.

GEORGE: *(Approaching public as though it were the girl)* Hey, Snow White. Want a bite of my apple?

GREG: *(Continues)* The creeping flow of her blood in me backs up a bit, and I can rest for a while—

DAVID: That-a-boy, Georgie. Show her your intellect.

GREG: —and stop fighting it. *(Beat)* So I hunt. It's
harmless, really. *(Strums barbed wire again and sings,
to the tune of "Oh, Susannah")*
Oh, Evalina, no llores mas por mi
(Stops, then starts again in English)
Oh Evalina, don't you cry for me
For I'm going on down to the border
With a six pack cross my knee.
(Laughs self-consciously, then speaks nervously to DAVID *as
he nears the car area)*
Make him get back in the car. She could pull a knife
on him. *(To public again)* I try not to hurt them, though,
especially the women.

DAVID: It's just like watching your V H S.

GREG: It's nothing personal. I mean, I loved my mother
and she was one of them. *(To his friends)* Shit, come on,
you guys. This isn't part of the deal. Can't you wait
until I'm done?

*(*GEORGE *gazes across the public then begins to crawl closer
as he "sees" the woman nearing the border.)*

DAVID: What's the matter, Greggie? Not getting the
attention you need?

GREG: *(Tries to get back to his story)* Especialmente las
mujeres, the women. Just want to *espantarlos un poco,*
scare them up a bit, let them know they don't belong
here. And we get ten bucks for each one we catch.
In a good week I can make seventy, eighty bucks.
Helps on the bills.

DAVID: Get lucky, baby. Heads or tails.

GREG: But, hey, let's lighten up now. *Vengan. Vengan.*
Loosen up. We'll pick up a bottle of rotgut tequila,
cruise on down to Dairy Mart road and shine the
brights on the wire, light 'em up, catch us some fish,
some *peces* for supper, huh?

(Huge groan from DAVID *in the car.* GREG *is disconcerted a moment.)*

(To DAVID*)* Fuck off. *(Beat)* I mean, we're all a mix, aren't we? *(Whispers)* But which half has got the heart, huh? Huh?

DAVID: Hey, Greg, how do you spell relief?

GREG: *(Oblivious to* DAVID's *interference)* Come on. You can get some relief. Take your mind off of a long day's work.

DAVID: Well?

GREG: *(To public)* So how do you spell relief?

*(*GEORGE *begins to caress the stage floor as he stares out at the woman that we can't see. He does this sensually, carefully.)*

DAVID: *(To* GEORGE*)* I spell it B-E-A-N-E-R-S.

GREG: Beaners.

*(*GREG *jumps back in the car.)*

DAVID: George will teach her the lesson she needs. She'll run back home now, tell her compadres: "You're playin' with fire, and you can be burned by fire...." *(To* GEORGE*)* What's the rest of the pledge, George? I'll knock ten dollars off your tab if you can remember it.

GEORGE: *(Remembering)* It goes.... It goes.... "can be burned by fire...and the...the...white man will rub two Mexicans together to make his fire."

GREG: *(Interrupts)* That's it. I'm walking. Get out of my fuckin' way.

DAVID: *(Grabs* GREG *by collar)* But old Ronald McDonald is going to score ninety billion and one tonight.

GREG: I'm calling Sharons.

DAVID: Can you smell the meat cooking, Greggie?
Or are you going to spoil your appetite again? *(Beat)*
Hey, give me that radio, you—

GREG: Calling for Officer Sharons. Calling for Officer—

DAVID: You idiot!

GREG: Emergency. A dozen beaners just broke the line
at fence number—

(DAVID hits GREG across the face with his gun.)

GREG: Fuck! You busted my goddamn nose.

DAVID: What has gotten into you?

GREG: I don't want things getting out of hand.

DAVID: You didn't mind things getting out of hand the
other night, though, did you?

GREG: That was different. This one's a kid.

DAVID: Sure, sure. Old Greggie coaching on the
sidelines. Grunt, grunt, grunt.

GREG: *(Motioning to gun)* O K. But you said you'd leave
that at home tonight. Give it to me.

DAVID: *(Calmly)* But it's my toy, Greg. And this is my
car. As a matter of fact, this is my brigade. I got us the
deal with the Feds, didn't I? Ten dollars a tag,
remember?

GREG: Get back in the fuckin' car, George.

DAVID: You're not very appreciative, Greg. I don't like
that in a man.

GREG: George!

DAVID: This is disappointing me, Greg.

GREG: We made a deal with the Feds we wouldn't
touch them anymore.

DAVID: George!

GEORGE: What? What? O K. Everything's cool. Don't get upset, Greg. *(Turns)* Look, she's fine. There she goes. I didn't touch her.

DAVID: Runnin' on back to Disneyland.

GEORGE: See? We can keep things in hand. It's cool.

GREG: Let's get out of here. This night is cracked.

GEORGE: Sure. Anything you say, Greg. We're all friends here, right?

GREG: Look. I want to have a good time too. Why do you two always have to fuck up my show?

DAVID: We'll be good little gentlemen from now on. Trust us, Greg.

GEORGE: Yeah. Trust us.

DAVID: *(Sneering)* And I apologize for slapping you. Really.

(Suddenly, DAVID throws himself on GEORGE's shoulder and begins, we think, to weep. GREG and GEORGE watch with concern. GEORGE is fooled.)

GEORGE: He's choked up.

DAVID: *(Through his gasping)* "This side is Mexican... the side with the heart..." Such a touching story, Greg.

GREG: Not bad, eh?

DAVID: There were times I thought I heard angels singing between the lines. *(Beat)* I mean, you're O K, Greg. *(Beat)* So, if it came down to it, down to the nitty-gritty, which would you choose, Birdseye's or Stouffer's?

GREG: I'm a canned foods man myself.

GEORGE: What's with the canned foods?

GREG: Shut up, George.

GEORGE: No.

DAVID: *(To GEORGE)* Take his advice, son, or you'll get your feelings hurt. *(To GREG)* Well?

GREG: Well?

GEORGE: Hey, I can make a balloon with my spit. *(He blows spit bubbles.)*

DAVID: Did they go for it?

GREG: I'm not sure.

DAVID: You're not sure? Every soldier must be sure.

GREG: That's right. No uncertainty. No doubts.

GEORGE: Come on, Greg. Is that true, the bit about your Dad and her molars?

GREG: Yep. But I threw in the part about him unbuttoning her shirt.

DAVID: So you fabricated?

GREG: Only in a minor way.

GEORGE: And your Dad, beaned to death with a dinner plate?

GREG: Nope. Cholesterol got him.

DAVID: He should have borrowed my rowing machine. *(Beat)* Shhh. Hear that, George?

(GEORGE shakes his head "no" while he listens.)

DAVID: Sounded like a howl.

GREG: No, David. You're a howl.

DAVID: That's the border wolf. It howls like that just before it kills.

GEORGE: I didn't hear a howl.

GREG: *(Joining in to get GEORGE)* I did. It sounded like this.

(GREG *springs up on car and howls. This should be more frightening than funny.*)

GREG: Well, how did I do?

DAVID: One minor criticism: your prose is a tad flat, somewhat backwards, too...working class. You've got to flex it up a bit.

GREG: You think so?

GEORGE: Can we quit early tonight? I need to call little bro.

DAVID: I'm sorry about Evalina.

GREG: Thanks.

DAVID: She was always nice to me when I came by your place for dinner. Once, she wiped the corners of my mouth with her apron. I think she appreciated my appetite. I always had a third helping.

GREG: You never met Evalina.

DAVID: You see how you restrict your imagination?

GEORGE: He's probably waiting up for me.

GREG: My imagination?

GEORGE: It's a nice thing to have someone waiting up for you.

GREG: *(Poking* DAVID *with his finger)* All you're good at is giving points, Mr Critic. Why don't you go stand out over there and see how many knives you can catch with your teeth. I caught three myself.

DAVID: Tsk, tsk. Do I detect a challenge? How infantile. But alright. *(He takes a dramatic breath, steps away from the car and faces the public.)* Alright. *(Calls)* Hello? Anyone at home? I know you're out there. And I'm calling especially to you sweet Yankee blue-bloods who belong on this side, not that one.... Look, I am going to give you a target, right inside here. *(He opens his mouth wide and hisses for some moments.)* Throw them right in here. Right in the bullseye. Or how about this? *(He turns his back to the public, spreads his arms and legs.)* Aim for the spine. Go ahead. Give me a tickle. *(Beat)* They're not interested in me, Greg. It's you they're lusting for. See? They won't tickle with me. *(Beat)* Alright then. *(Spins around)* Then I'll tickle with you. *(Beat)* Want to see me do an imitation of a baby radish with its roots growing?

GREG: A radish *is* a root.

DAVID: But the root has got roots as well and they crawl deep in the dark, like this.

(DAVID squirms about. He is serious about doing a good imitation. He begins to make hissing sounds also. GREG and GEORGE remain in or around the car area.)

DAVID: Listen! Listen! You can hear them growing...radish roots. They make a sound when they grow— *(Makes a sound)* —radiating out minute bits of heat into the wet dirt, making the wet dirt hiss. *(Makes hissing noises)* Hot in the mouth! The tongue burning. My sister and I. We'd fill up our mouths, see who could chew up the most before we spit them out like confetti, all over our shoes. *(Beat)* When my mother tried to leave, I said to her: "Mother, you're an insect, and, like the child you brought me up to be, I'll pluck out your wings." *(Beat)* After Sis passed away, I couldn't apologize about the radishes. I had wanted to send Sis a nice card, some chocolates, maybe a balloon. She was an intelligent girl. When she left home, she said to me: "I'm root-bound here. And now I've got to crack my pot." *(Laughs nervously)* Telephone pole cracked her pot too, you could say. *(Pretends to write a letter in the air)*

GREG: *(Sees a child in the distance)* Check this out: a toddler.

GEORGE: *(Yells)* Hey, kiddo, *(Whistles)* want to play Master of the Universe?

DAVID: Dear Sis: Sorry about the radishes. Love, Bro. *(Takes off his shoe, polishes it on his thigh, and carefully lines it up on the stage floor)*

GREG: Nope. Headin' his fanny back to them hills.

GEORGE: *(Motioning towards DAVID)* He's strippin' again.

GREG: This is getting to be a yawn, David.

DAVID: *(Ignoring them)* Now, my mother was what you might call a...call a... *(Snaps his fingers until his friends give him his line)*

GREG: ...a dignified type.

DAVID: *(Continues)* ...call a...dignified type of insect, like the mantis. Her wings. Just wouldn't give, not matter how hard you tugged. One day my mother is making me P B J's three stacks high. The next day she's taking off her apron, balling it up, shoving it down the compactor, walking out. When I tackled her on the lawn, asked her why, she said I was old enough to take care of myself, that she was growing weary of the sight of me. She gave me a look then, the way a hole looks back at you if you're looking down in it. And then I knew she knew about Sis. *(Takes off other shoe, polishes it, and lines it up carefully next to the other one)*

DAVID: My Daddy had a saying: Never... Never... *(He can't remember his lines.)* Fuck!

GREG: Never shut your eyes.

DAVID: Never shut your eyes to a woman...because if you do, before you know it, she'll stick you full like a pin cushion, sew your scrotum to your ass, use you for a foot stool. *(Takes off one sock, lays it gently beside a shoe)* Radishes. A shame they ever existed. *(Beat)* I could have plucked out their wings like insects. But they wouldn't.

Stand still. They squirm. They wiggle. They wreak
havoc in your garden. *(Removes other sock. Notices bare
feet and wiggles them in fascination.)* Hey. You got to keep
fit. If the body is a drag... *(Snaps fingers. No response.
Snaps them again.)*

GREG: Learn the shit, will you, David.

DAVID: Show some consideration, please?

GREG: *(Wearily)* If the body is a drag, the spirit's
gonna— *(Sticks his finger in his mouth and gags)*

DAVID: —the spirit will gag. *(Sits down and begins to row)*
Row, row, row your boat
Gently down the stream
Merrily, merrily, merrily, merrily
Life is but a
(Draws out last note)
Radish!
(Quits rowing. Gets up and unbuttons his shirt.)

GEORGE: *(To GREG)* How much you think they're
paying for this peep show?

DAVID: I mean, when you grow up you've got choices
to make in life. So you choose: Johnny Carson or
Hee-Haw, Seven-Up or Sprite, C B S or N B C, Beechnut
or Juicy Fruit, Trident or Dentine. *(Beat)* I had a fiancée
once. But every time I desired her and leaned to deliver
the first real kiss of my life, this music began in my ear
(Sings):
Wrigley Spearmint gum, gum, gum
Wrigley Spearmint gum, gum, gum

*(As he repeats these lines, GREG and GEORGE sing the
accompaniment to the song "Carry it with you... That great
fresh flavor" until DAVID silences them with his arms,
as a conductor of an orchestra would.)*

DAVID: Excuse me, gentlemen, but I like to do it solo.
(Beat) Somehow the melody put me off kissing her. Or

I'd reach in her shirt to fondle her breast and whisper
bits of sassyfras into her ear, but instead I'd start *(Sings)*
Gettin' that barefoot feelin'
Drinkin' Mountain Dew
(Laughs wildly as though tickled. Then speaks seriously.)
When things get hot, cool is all you got. *(Beat)* I couldn't
get that music out of my brain. *(Beat)* I work for a
law firm. *(Lays shirt out on floor and kneels to button
it up again)* My partner says he likes girls in their
adolescence. My father liked them young too, but he
swore sheep had the greater dignity. He brought a girl
home for me once when I made an A in Mathematics.
And the three of us got drunk. *(Laughs)* All I remember
are three white hooves and one black one. *(Stands and
sings in opera style)*
Baa-baa black sheep
Can I tickle your wool?
I've only been arrested once. After Sis's funeral.
I went out hacking up neighbor's gardens, hunting
for radishes. This officer picked me up, along with this
Chicano teen from downtown. At the jail he thought I'd
passed out. She was fighting like a whirlwind, so he put
a gag on her in the cell adjacent to mine and pulled off
her trousers. I could see the girl's face. She was trying to
scream, but the gag wouldn't let her. The officer was so
busy with her he didn't see me reach my arm through
the bars and touch her face. She had hair that curled
like Sis's. Come on, I whispered to her, scream, scream,
damn you. And her whole face was screaming, only no
sound was coming out, and I felt like someone pulled
my plug, because I started to scream instead: *(Whispers)*
No! No! and I kept on screaming until the officer put
out my lights.

GREG: There! George! There's two of them!

GEORGE: Where? I can't see anything.

GREG: Right there! Look... Nope. Lost them. Damn.

DAVID: Then I dreamt about Sis, both of us up to our wrists in the dirt, fishing for radishes in the garden. Like a pearl in an oyster, she'd say, when she pulled one up out of the dirt. *(Beat)*....She was my...my.... *(Snaps fingers. No response.)* Hey!

GEORGE & GREG: Fuck you!

DAVID: She was my...friend. *(Takes off britches, lays them out. The shape of a person is now laid out on the floor.)*

GREG: Not the all-cotton Armani trousers.

DAVID: *(Playfully)* Now, which one is me? This one? *(To self)* or that one? *(To suit on floor)* Or is that old Sis lying there? *(Beat)* Sis and I were from an aspiring middle class neighborhood. Even as kids we were smart enough to keep our eyes on the next rung of the ladder.

(While DAVID tells the following, GEORGE crawls into DAVID's space, climbs onto the clothes and does push-ups over them.)

DAVID: Naturally, we hung around the top of the cream neighborhood parks so we could mingle with the best. I mean, in our town we were the "betters", but we aspired to be the best. Well, some of the kids we met there started calling me a pussy for hanging out with my sister. I was twelve and she was ten. They said I could join their club but that I'd have to choose, them or her. Of course I said I'd choose them, because I knew I could make it up to Sis later when we got home.

(Now GEORGE flips over on his back and is motionless. DAVID stands over him.)

DAVID: But then they gave me a dare in order to join. And they held her down.

(Kneels over GEORGE's body. GEORGE is lifeless.)

DAVID: They pulled up her skirt. They dared me. If you say no to a dare, you're a pussy. I could not be a pussy.

But everything was getting sort of out of focus. I took
the radishes out of my pocket. I had three of them,
big as chestnuts that she and I dug that morning.
I put them inside her.

(DAVID *kicks* GEORGE *hard in the side, but he does this with
no apparent emotion.*)

DAVID: I put them inside her. She just kept whispering
my name. She wouldn't scream. Just saying, (*Whispers*)
"David, no. David, no. David, no. David, no."

(GEORGE *moves out of* DAVID's *"show".*)

DAVID: She never looked me in the face again, for
eleven years, until her Toyota hit that telephone post.
Then she had to look at me. Lying in that coffin, she
had no choice but to look up at me. (*Speaks to clothes
on floor*) "I'm sorry, Sis", I said. (*Speaks each word in
isolation*) I am sorry. (*After a moment, spits on the face of
the clothes figure on the stage floor. But this action is almost
tender.*) Insects. Insects we were. And they plucked out
our wings. (*Beat*) I'm not pulling your leg like Greg
was. See, when you break a human being in half, right
over your knee, crack, like a stick, there is no fixing
him. Like there was no fixing her, my little sis.

(*Covers face with hands as in a moment of agony, but then he
is laughing.* GREG *walks into* DAVID's *space.*)

GREG: Come on, come on. *Rapido, rapido.* "Bingo," goes
la cabeza: David, you knock off wets for a kick, because
you feel guilty about the...let's call it the vegetable rape
of your *pobre hermana*. Go ahead, put yourself in the
frame. Frame the pig.

DAVID: It was misplaced anger, transfer of violence,
all due to a dysfunctional home.

GREG: It feels better, doesn't it, once you get a handle on
the *problema*?

DAVID: I appreciate the kindness, Greg, but get the sweet Jesus out of my gig.

GREG: *(Returning to car)* You're not living up to your degree, David.

DAVID: Certainly I am *(Beat)* regretful about Sis. *(Makes popping sounds)* Fried my soul. But it isn't her at all. I'm tired of my job at the law firm. I'm bored. *(Beat)* There are just too many decisions to make: Mustard vinaigrette or the house special? B M W or Volvo? Paper or plastic?

(DAVID suddenly gags and begins to choke. GREG watches with disdain, but GEORGE is fooled. He cautiously approaches DAVID while glancing with fear at border.)

GEORGE: *(Whispers)* David?

(DAVID continues to gag.)

GEORGE: David? Are you O K? *(To GREG)* Something's the matter with him, Greg. Come and look.

(GEORGE touches DAVID with his foot. DAVID doesn't move. Then, suddenly, he grabs GEORGE's leg and bites it. GEORGE screams and shakes him loose. GREG and DAVID laugh together. Then DAVID looks around him.)

DAVID: Oh, no. Did I fall on my sapling?

GREG: I hope so.

GEORGE: That wasn't funny. I'm going home. Even if I have to walk.

(DAVID gets up and approaches GEORGE. DAVID spits on his hands and smooths GEORGE's hair back in place. This is a tender action. Then he suddenly strikes him.)

GEORGE: Hey!

DAVID: Remember our agreement? The three of us stick together. Right, George? Right?

(GEORGE *doesn't answer.*)

GREG: Lay off him.

DAVID: What?

GREG: I said lay off him.

DAVID: What did Greg say?

GREG: Greg said "Fuck you."

DAVID: (*Takes a moment to register this, then sings at* GREG)
On the border, Greg's getting nauseous.
On the border, he's just too serious.

GREG: (*Pushing* DAVID *backwards with the lines that he sings*)
On the border, you're playing frat-boy-king.
On the border, your education's nothing.

DAVID: (*Pushes Greg back with his lines as he sings*)
On the border, it's your American half-dream
One side upriver, the other downstream.

GREG: (GREG *is winning*)
On the border, too many tricks in your head
On the border, you just might wind up dead.

(*There is a silence for some moments as* GREG *and* GEORGE *stare at one another. Then* GEORGE *begins applauding and continues until he gets their attention. Then* DAVID *grins and casually picks his clothes up off the floor and slings over his shoulder. He crosses to the car and* GREG *follows him.*)

GEORGE: What a show!

DAVID: You liked that, didn't you?

GREG: I'd never have guessed.

GEORGE: You are a poet.

DAVID: Ah, but a poet born from grief. And everyone believes a poet, especially a poet who...

GEORGE: I had to memorize a poem once for class.

DAVID: ...indulges a little, elaborates a bit for the show.

GEORGE: Want to hear me recite it?

GREG: So the radishes were only an elaboration?

DAVID: Only an elaboration?

GEORGE: The poem I learnt was about an idiot who sawed off his arm.

GREG: So you lied.

DAVID: The radish episode is true.

GEORGE: I just got to say that that was a pretty disgusting thing to do to your sister, David.

(DAVID *shrugs*.)

GREG: I'm sorry about your sister. She always had a nice word for me.

DAVID: *(Casually)* You never met her.

(GREG *shrugs*.)

GEORGE: Do you think they're sorry?

(Motions to border)

DAVID: *(Whispers)* Frankly, dear, I don't give a damn.

GREG: So what did you choose in the end?

DAVID: Why, I choose Marlboro, Of course.

(DAVID *and* GREG *laugh together, as though to an inside joke.*)

GEORGE: *(Angered)* You two are so cool, aren't you? Big jokers with broken hearts.

DAVID: *(Looking at his watch)* It's time to move fence lines.

GREG: Yep. *Los peces* aren't biting here.

GEORGE: Well, I can do it too, you know.

DAVID: You've got asparagus for brains, Georgie. I said let's go.

GEORGE: You just watch. Old George will surprise you. *(He moves across stage, whistling and glancing shyly at the border/public.)*

DAVID: *(Claps softly)* That was wonderful, George, now zip your fly and let's go.

GEORGE: *(Confiding)* But it's different for me, 'cause mine is a secret.

DAVID: George. Old buddy. You're just blocking the view.

GREG: Shhh. George has a secret. Mustn't tell. Mustn't tell.

DAVID: Alright. But there's nothing that long-toothed border wolf hates more than a pitiful performance.

(GREG and DAVID howl.)

GEORGE: Just ignore them. *(Beat)* Lookie what I can do? *(Grabs barbed wire and twists it. Holds his hands up.)* See? *(Beat)* You got to forgive them. They want to be honest. They're O K guys. I grew up with them.

DAVID: This is a warning, George. If you step on that sapling... Move it. To the right.

(GEORGE does so.)

DAVID: Farther. Farther.

GREG: Farther.

GEORGE: *(Moves closer to public)* Is this O K? *(Beat)* I don't want them to hear some of this, so I got to speak soft. I was a kid when it started growing. It was the size of a penny, right in the middle of my back. It just popped up one day when I was standing in front of this billboard waiting for the school bus. On the billboard was a picture of a camel, sitting on a beach with sunglasses, smoking a cigarette. The camel had this smile on his face I'd never seen on any human face before: this smile of slap-happiness, of some just-do-it secret. And that's when I felt it pop up on my back: the hump. The camel's hump. *(Does a curious rotating motion with his shoulders)* Most kids would have got scared, but I wasn't surprised. I just kept it hid under my jacket so as not to scare my friends. *(Beat)* By the time I was a grown man I had a genuine camel's hump on my back.

GREG: His fuckin' hump again.

GEORGE: When it quit growing I started waiting in front of the mirror for the rest of it, for the smile. I was patient, too. But it didn't come. I started smokin' two at a time, to hurry it up a bit but the smile still held out on me. So there I was, a camel's hump without a smile, like a dick without balls. *(Itches his back)* Don't believe me? *(Turns around and lifts his shirt. We see nothing.)* Then what the hell is that? A pimple the size of a pup?

DAVID: It's an infected pore.

GREG: Another stripper. Yawn.

DAVID: Hey! Look out. I saw something move over there.

GEORGE: *(Pulls down shirt fast)* Don't touch. It's *my* hump. *(Beat)* Now my Daddy, he had—

DAVID: Not another father story.

GEORGE: —no hump, no smile, and, after the mines, only one lung to smoke with. But he was a G-O-O-D man. *(Beat)* I was into four-legged animals back then, so he took me hunting. I was seven. We sat on the tail of the truck, oiling the rifles. It was so cold I couldn't feel my hands in my gloves. I walked behind him. I must have stepped on every damn twig in the woods. He kept smacking the cap off my head— *(Smacks self in head a few times)* —telling me to shush up. Finally, we saw one. A buck. He was the size of a horse with antlers like Christmas trees. *(Dramatically)* His breath circled up out of his nose like ropes. *(Snickers at friends in car area)* Not bad, huh?

DAVID: George, I sense another boredom riot. If you don't pick up the rhythm, we might have to cancel. How about a questionnaire to liven things up? Let's see a show of hands. How many of you have enjoyed—

GEORGE: Shut up.

DAVID: *(Continues)* —a Big Mac so conscientiously that you had to hurry off to the restroom after the meal to beat off?

(Not to be discouraged, GEORGE returns to his monologue)

GEORGE: My Daddy whispered : *(Shouts)* "If you make a noise, I'll kill you." The barrel rose over my.... No... How about this: The cold, black barrel rose over my Daddy's shoulder—

DAVID: *(As though counting hands)* Which of you had the guts to switch from Coke to Pepsi out of respect for Schwarzkopf?

(GEORGE now raises the invisible rifle and aims it at his friends.)

GEORGE: —and he took aim. The buck raised its head. Its long tongue licked its grey nose. And then I saw it. *(Does so)* Wham. For the second, maybe last time in my life, that smile, that smirk of oblivion and party time. And then it hit me: That was my camel. Not a buck but my camel. *(Lets out a wild yodel)* That's just what I did. Then that camel burned rubber. The shot rang out. My father spun, and out went my lights.

GREG: This one's especially for you, David: Do you recycle? *(Beat)* Only your milk jugs? Tsk, tsk.

DAVID: *(To GREG)* You don't respect your environment.

GEORGE: When I woke I saw leaves above me, then my Daddy's face, the spit dripping down his chin, right into my eye. He made me crawl back to the truck on my hands and knees, with the barrel of his gun at my ass. But I didn't mind a bit. I was happy. My camel had got away. And I'd been born again by that smile. *(Beat)* Watch this. *(Walks and chews like a camel)*

DAVID: Hey, Greg, were you S D S S? *(Whispers)* Rat-tat-tat-tat. I was.

GREG: *(Whispers)* Secret Desert Storm Supporter? You know, David, that's what I've always appreciated about you liberal types. I mean, recycling not only your clear glass but your green glass as well.

GEORGE: Beautiful, huh? That stride. The stride of a camel. There is nothing else like it.

DAVID: Hey, I care, while you, you've made no choices for the future.

GEORGE: I paste billboards now, and take care of my little bro. But don't think I'm one of those broken-hearted give-ups. I'm watching out for that smile again. You see, unless you are a certain kind of American, you miss the smile, and all those people out there, sneaking their way in here, are out to steal that smile. But over my dead body. That's what I say: over my dead body. *(Itches hump furiously)* It's a sport. *(Beat)* Want another peek at my hump? *(Begins to lift shirt teasingly)* Fuck off. Go get your own. *(Beat)* I'm a camel. *(Chews again)*

(DAVID moves in on GEORGE's space. He pushes GEORGE onto all fours and puts his foot on GEORGE's back. GEORGE doesn't resist.)

DAVID: You, sir, are obviously malfunctioning.
Your father shoved a gun barrel up your rectum,
so you are also anal retentive.

GEORGE: Anal what?

DAVID: And if a gentleman such as this is anal, it only
follows that he'll work the border.

GEORGE: Oink, oink.

DAVID: I never saw a yellow ribbon tied around your
tree, George. And I know for a fact that you don't save
your newspapers. Did you know that it takes ten years
for a seed to become a sapling?

GEORGE: *(Shouts)* This is my story. Mine. Get the fuck
out!

GREG: *(To DAVID)* You know, David, this is what gets
me. How come you always get to interrupt? Whenever
you want?

DAVID: Because you let me?

GEORGE: *(Struggles to his feet)* Fuckin' traitors. Both of
you. You're no better than a pair of beaners. Fuckin'
beaners, both of you.

DAVID: *(Beat)* George, Greg. This is why I must
constantly interrupt you.

It's my duty. You see, people like me, we don't call
them beaners, wetbacks, or greasers. We who aren't
of your, shall we say "constipated class", we call them
illegal aliens, immigration offenders, or, for those of us,
like myself, still religiously inclined, "poor souls". Try
and show a little understanding. I mean, I've used my
education to figure it out: We stagnate their economies
with our I M Fs and can't-pay-them-off-ever loans, so
they've got to try and cross and work for Roto-Rooter.
Why can't you two be a little more sympathetic?
Citizens like myself are trying hard to *(Sings)* reach out

and touch someone? This tree, for instance.
(He kneels beside the sapling, sings.)
I'm the Robin Hood of Saplings
I watch over the small trees
And when I see one broken
It brings me to my knees.
(Beat) At the end of the day, you're still an ignorant
man, George, and so are you, Greg, sorry. You don't
care about the future, about the air the children of
tomorrow will need to breathe. You're selfish, poor,
a measly excuse for a working class.

GEORGE: Fuck you. I'm upper working class.

*(DAVID returns to GEORGE, smacks GEORGE across the
face at each word. He does this with measured boredom,
and GEORGE is passive.)*

DAVID: You *(Smack)* poor, *(Smack)* ignorant *(Smack)*
bigot. *(Beat)* Feel any better?

(GEORGE nods.)

DAVID: I understand you, George. Your psychological
makeup is painfully clear. Nevertheless, you deserve
to be punished, as you went ahead and did your show
against my better judgment. You're going to have to
drag.

GREG: No.

DAVID: George?

GEORGE: I don't want to. It hurts.

DAVID: Learning is painful. *(He takes a small piece of wire
from his pocket.)* Open your mouth, George.

GREG: I said no.

DAVID: I heard you. A powerful word, isn't it? "No."
"No." "No." Though it depends on who's saying
it.*(Beat)* I'm not correcting you, Greg. I'm correcting
George.

GREG: I don't want blood on my shirt. That's my shirt he's wearing.

DAVID: Take off the shirt, George.

(GEORGE *does so after a moment's reluctance.*)

GREG: Put it back on, George.

(GEORGE *starts to.*)

DAVID: George.

GEORGE: I don't want to drag. It hurts.

GREG: Get back in the car, George.

(No one moves.)

GREG: Not tonight, David. Just this once, do me a favor. I don't think I've asked for one in a while.

DAVID: *(After a silence)* Put the shirt back on, George.

GREG: Thanks. I mean it. Thanks. *(Beat)* Thanks, thanks, thanks. Why am I always thanking you? You pull this every time. Why do you get to decide when and how we do our stuff, where we have to stand?

DAVID: *(Ignores GREG)* No drag, got it, George? But repeat after me: "I am the ignorant one—"

GEORGE: *(Repeats with toleration rather than obedience)* "I am the ignorant one—"

DAVID: "—the humped one—"

GEORGE: "—the humped one—"

DAVID: "—the...the..." *(Snaps his fingers so GREG will give him his line)* Isn't anyone helping out anymore?

GREG: Looks like things are going to hell pretty quick, heh, David?

GEORGE: *(Screams)* I want to finish my story!

DAVID: I give up.

GEORGE: So I hunt Mexicans. It's not a personal thing. Why should I like them? *(Turns to* DAVID*)* But I like you. You wear nice clothes. You let me mow your lawn.

DAVID: *(Sniffs under his arms)* My armpits are odor free.

GREG: You don't itch your crotch in public.

GEORGE: I mean, how could I hate you when you gave me your old Adidas and bought my flag for me at K-Mart?

DAVID: So there are no inappropriate feelings?

*(*GREG *shrugs.)*

GEORGE: Naw. *(Beat)* Well, how did you like it?

(They ignore him.)

DAVID: *(To* GREG*)* It's ten o'clock.

GREG: Shut up, George. Let's shift.

GEORGE: Just a fuckin' minute. After you guys went you got some fuckin' feedback. It's my turn now. I get my minute in the sun.

DAVID: But really, Georgie, a camel?

GEORGE: Yeah. A camel.

GREG: *(Laughing now with* DAVID*)* A camel? I'm tired of this. It's time to move.

GEORGE: Yeah. A camel. Is a camel worth any less than a radish? Than a half-breed with a heart split in two?

DAVID: Have you ever stopped to consider the size of a camel's turd?

GEORGE: O K, O K. But you guys are screwed, because my camel could eat your radish any day. But, you know, I had a rhythm going, and you just moved in, without even asking, and fucked it up.

GREG: You're pathetic, George. You didn't have a
rhythm going. You never had a rhythm going.

DAVID: Don't be too hard on him. He's mentally
challenged.

GREG: *(Turns on* DAVID*)* Is he? Well, let's not forget
you're only hanging out with us, Mr Educado, due to
our good graces. But you know, I think it's time we sent
you back to your hot tub.

DAVID: Please. Not that. Let me stay with you fellows.
Let me get some dirt on my boots, some oil under my
fingernails.

GREG: I've been thinking. All these years I wanted to
ask you, but I figured better not because you're my
friend. But I want to know. Now. What else? What else
from the root family, huh, David? Is it only radishes,
or do you get hot over tubers as well? Most of all,
did you have the guts to try them out on yourself
before you did your sister in?

GEORGE: What's a tuber?

DAVID: A tuber is a situation like this one. Stuck in the
ground with no place to grow. Snore, snore. You two
Boy Scouts are getting so predictable I'm going to have
to go back to playing tennis at the club.

GREG: *(Sniffs* DAVID*)* You know, I've never liked the
way you smell.

DAVID: You mean I've practiced all these years for
nothing?

GEORGE: What the fuck is up here?

DAVID: Did I ever mention to you two that I finally
hired myself a maid?

GEORGE: A beaner?

DAVID: Only the best. Guess what I named her, Greg?

GREG: Maid.

DAVID: Getting warmer.

GEORGE: Cleanie-beanie?

DAVID: Colder.

GREG: I'll tell you what the difference is, David.
Like all of them in your club: You wear deodorant,
but you can't hide the stink. A real handicap.

DAVID: I gave her a special name. *(Beat)* In honor of
Greg, of course.

GEORGE: You see, Greg? He likes you. *(Beat)* Watch this
trick: I can eat a rock.

GREG: No. No. I don't want to see you eat a rock. I don't
want to see you swallow a beer cap. I don't want to see
you put a centipede down your pants. Stop trying to
act like a funny guy. You're no more worthless than the
rest of us.

GEORGE: I'm not?

GREG: No, you're smart. Sometimes.

GEORGE: I am?

DAVID: This is.... This is.... Words fail me.

GREG: As a matter of fact, you're a winner.

GEORGE: A winner?

GREG: Who spots the most beaners on a weekly basis?

GEORGE: Me?

GREG: Yes. You. Who spots the least?

GEORGE: David.

GREG: And you know why? Because he gets paid not
only for the beaners he turns in, but for the ones he lets
cross.

GEORGE: Lets cross?

DAVID: Greg.

GREG: As a matter of fact, he gets paid a bonus for the athletic types he lets through. The ones that can do the hard labor.

GEORGE: *(To* DAVID*)* That's not true, is it, David?

DAVID: Hey Greg. About that money you owe me.

GEORGE: You get paid for letting them cross?

DAVID: I think I'll need it by tomorrow.

GEORGE: Why? Why?

GREG: Because David knows he's got to let in just enough beaners to work dead cheap so he can—

DAVID: —maintain my standard of living? It's a very good standard, too. Don't forget it.

GEORGE: I can't believe this.

DAVID: But there's another reason you've left out, Greg. I want to share.

GREG: Share?

DAVID: Certainly. This is the melting pot, isn't it? If we keep everyone out, we'll lose the mix.

GEORGE: You lied to me, David. You never did that to me before.

DAVID: So has Greg. He knew all about it.

GEORGE: Greg?

GREG: If it weren't for David, we wouldn't even have the deal with the Feds to begin with.

GEORGE: Well, fuck you. Fuck you both, I'm going home.

DAVID: *(Takes* GEORGE'*s face in his hands)* Hey, I'm still
your friend. I've taken good enough care of you so far,
haven't I? Who helped you out on your electric bill last
month? *(Beat)* You see? I'm still your friend.

*(*GEORGE *pulls away, but less angry now.)*

DAVID: That's right. I am. And I'll tell you what. Just
to show you I'm respectable about it, I'm inviting you
over so you can finger my new maid's teeth. It will
tickle your innards. No charge.

GREG: You really fell for that molar story, didn't you,
you *hijo de la gran puta,* son of a bitch.

DAVID: Something tells me that lately you've begun to
feel uncomfortable about our relationship.

GREG: No. This isn't a friendship thing. We've always
been amigos. Father, Son, and the Holy Ghost, right?

GEORGE: I want to be the ghost. Hey! Look! There's
three of them!

*(*DAVID *pays no attention to* GEORGE, *but* GREG *is torn
between going to help* GEORGE *and confronting* DAVID.)*

DAVID: Then Simon says, "What is it?"

GEORGE: Oh, shit. They're going to charge. Come on,
Greg!

GREG: It's how you like it out here.

GEORGE: I like it out here. *(To border)* Go back! Go back!
We're not ready for you!

DAVID: Oh, please. Are we going to have another
"David thinks he's got gold for shit and only hangs
out with us, hoping it will rub off" episodes? Or how
about the rerun where you curse me and George for
feeling up the chicks we catch just because you haven't
got the stomach to join in.

GREG: I never wanted to join in. I just wanted the ten bucks a hit.

GEORGE: Will you two cut the shit and look alive before we lose these guys?

DAVID: Shut up, George. *(To* GREG*)* Or perhaps you never joined in because of the difficulty you have in getting an erection that will last more than three seconds.

GEORGE: I don't want to talk about Greg's dick!

GREG: *(Refuses to let* DAVID *"get" him)* If the Feds ever changed their minds, if they ever wanted to burn us...

GEORGE: They fucking crossed.

DAVID: You think they don't know what we're up to? You really are confused.

GEORGE: A hundred feet away from us and we're letting them cross. That's thirty bucks down the drain.

GREG: Well, if they ever did decide to burn us, they'd burn me and George, not you. Not you, because you've got a Lawn-boy rider and a concrete pool.

GEORGE: Let's talk about my show. I want to talk about it!

DAVID: *(To* GREG*)* My, you are breathing rapidly. You must be ill. Should we call it quits for the night? But we still haven't guessed what I named my maid? *(No response from* GREG*)* I named her Evalina. *(Beat)* I did it for you. And all I get in return is a—

GREG: *(Interrupts)* You named your maid Evalina? Evalina? Is she one of the chosen ones you let through? I bet she loves her job, doesn't she, cleaning your toilet the same way she brushes her teeth?

DAVID: Teeth. Teeth. It's got into your subconscious, hasn't it, son?

GREG: Tell us how you caught her, David, tell us what you said to her to make her feel safe. Tell us. Which fence line?

DAVID: You're tiresome.

GREG: Did she walk across or did she crawl? What was it like? Hey, David, was it like this?

(GREG *crawls from the border. Though he pretends to be a Mexican woman, it is important that his voice is not affected. He does not try to "sound" like a woman but speaks with his own voice. He may affect a slight accent but then drop it when the action gets more violent.*)

GREG: Hallo! Hallo! Gringo. Do you have a job for me? Gringo. Gringo. Can you help me?

(*As* GREG *speaks,* DAVID *begins to circle* GREG, *joining in the game.*)

DAVID: How can I help you, miss?

GREG: Oh, Mister Gringo. I want to work. I like work.

(DAVID *trips* GREG *and pushes him to his knees.*)

DAVID: So you like to work?

(GEORGE *gets into the game.* DAVID *and* GEORGE *both interrogate* GREG.)

GEORGE: What kind of work?

GREG: Anything. I need money. *Dinero. Dinero.*

DAVID: What for?

GEORGE: What for?

GREG: For pretty clothes?

DAVID: (*Smacks* GREG *in the head*) Stupid answer. Try again. Why do you want money?

GREG: I'm hungry. (*Beat*) I'm starving.

GEORGE: *(Picks up a handful of dirt)* Then open up.
I got a McDonald's for you.

(GEORGE forces dirt in GREG's mouth. GREG spits it out and attempts to rise. DAVID forces him back onto his knees.)

DAVID: So you want me to give you a job, heh, sweetheart? Why don't you get a nice job in your own hometown?

GEORGE: *(Kicks him)* Yeah. Why do you want to come over here and take mine?

DAVID: You better answer old George, miss, or he'll throw you to the border wolf. *(Beat)* Answer him, you bitch!

GREG: Because... Because...

DAVID: Answer him.

GREG: Because there's no jobs in my hometown.
The Yankee pays better over here than the Yankee does over there. *(Beat) Putas. Todos los* Yankees.

DAVID: Did you hear that, George? Cursed at me in Mexican. The bitch.

(DAVID slaps GREG.)

GEORGE: The bitch.

DAVID: But I'm a nice guy. I'll give you a job. You can come home with me. But are you clean?

(GREG holds up his hands to show DAVID that his hands are clean.)

DAVID: Not your hands. I mean what you've got between your legs. Show me.

GREG: No.

GEORGE: Show us.

GREG: No.

GEORGE & DAVID: Show us!

GREG: No!

(DAVID *throws* GREG *on his back and straddles him.*
GEORGE *pins* GREG'*s arms down and puts his hand*
over GREG'*s mouth so* GREG *can't speak.*)

DAVID: So you want a job? Well, if you're going to
work for me, you can't wear those dirty shirts.

(*He rips* GREG'*s shirt open.* GREG *struggles.*)

GEORGE: Nice tits. Look at her tits.

DAVID: What's a girl like you doing in a mess like this?
But I will have to give you a tip for your troubles.

(*He takes out some dollar bills and stuffs them in* GREG'*s*
mouth so GREG *can't speak.*)

GEORGE: Touch her, David. Hurt her. Twist her tit.

(DAVID *twists* GREG'*s nipple and* GREG *screams through*
the bills.)

DAVID: It's not nice to shout.

(GREG *struggles and manages to throw* DAVID *off of him.*
Now GREG *sits on* DAVID. GEORGE *has backed off.* GREG
spits the bills at DAVID'*s face. There are some moments of*
silence as DAVID *and* GREG *become aware of their new*
positions.)

GREG: So you want a job, huh? (*Strikes him hard*)
I'm talking to you. You want a job?

GEORGE: Do it again, Greg.

(GREG *strikes* DAVID *again.*)

GREG: Well, if you're going to work for me, you can't
wear those fancy shirts.

(*Rips* DAVID'*s shirt open.* DAVID *is passive, as though*
stunned.)

GREG: Nice, *chica*. Really nice. Here in America—

(GEORGE *pulls on* DAVID's *hair and spits on him.*)

GREG: —we know how to appreciate a nice piece of foreign work. *(Beat)* How does it feel, baby? How does it feel to be on the bottom, with your ass in the dirt? Want to come home with me and scrub my tub? I'll buy you a green apron.

(Some moments of silence)

(As DAVID *speaks the following,* GREG's *power leaves him.)*

DAVID: You know, Greg, I've been meaning to ask you— *(Beat)* —did you ever get that G E D diploma you were working for? You really should, you know. Not that there's anything wrong with not even having a high school diploma, but it is important to be an educated man. That way, you've got more choices. ꦴ You can move up in the world.

(DAVID *pushes* GREG *off of him.* DAVID *cleans himself off. Neither* GEORGE *nor* GREG *resists him. Then he notices the sapling.)*

DAVID: You fucking clodhoppers. I can't believe it. You stepped on my sapling. Squashed it.

GEORGE: I didn't do it. Greg stepped on it. He did it.

DAVID: Broke its back. You sons of bitches. With your big, dirty, stinking boots. *(Beat)* This night is over. We're calling it quits.

GEORGE: *(Yells)* But I want to have a good time!

GREG: *(Calmly, not shouting)* Aren't you? Aren't you having a good time, George?

DAVID: *(Gazing at sapling)* I don't like to see things die. *(Beat)* Do you remember the taste of your first girl, Greg?

GREG: No. I don't.

DAVID: But you must. How can anyone not remember the taste of their first girl, when you're leaning over to kiss her...

GREG: I don't remember.

DAVID: ...when you're leaning over to kiss her, and her mouth is shining like glass, and her chest is rising and falling when she breathes, rising and falling like the wing of a bird. *(Beat)* But then you hear it again. And it stops you cold. *(He begins to sing.)*
Wrigley Spearmint Radish, Radish, Radish.
Wrigley Spearmint Radish, Radish, Radish.

(GREG watches him some moments, then begins to shout at DAVID until he drowns DAVID out. Then GREG continues.)

GREG: Stop. Stop it. Just stop it. *(Beat)* You think that's how it happens? Yeah? You think that's what I remember when I remember my first girl? No, I remember this:

(He slowly, gently runs his finger over DAVID's lip. DAVID does not move or respond.)

GREG: Evalina. She used to run her finger over my lip like that, and then there was no better place to be than right there where she touched me. *(After a moment of silence, he moves away.)* But that's not how the story gets told, is it, David? Well, I'll tell you right now that I can one-up your radish, you mother fucker. Just watch this. *(Turns to public again, starts out speaking fast)* Hey! Hey! *Dame dos cuchillos.* Throw me a couple of knives. Right here. Think I haven't got it in me? Well, half of me is *mejicano.* The other half of me is WASP. *Come sabes* which side is which? My mother used to tell me: "*Este lado es mejicano.* This side is Mexican, *(Slaps left breast)* the side with the heart." *(Beat)* My father made O K *dinero.* He helped me get a loan on my car. *(Turns to DAVID)* Are you listening? *(Back to public/border)* I met

my first girl when I was working at the grocers on 17th
and Chestnut. She was a chicana.

DAVID: *(Shoves him)* You already told us your *(Beat)*
emotional dentistry saga, Greg. No second chances.

GREG: *(Shoves him back)* I figured, like father, like son.
And she was legal, nice trailer, two-parent family. *(Beat)*
Then she got pregnant. I brought her home to meet my
Father.

GEORGE: Hey, I didn't get a second shot. This isn't fair.
This isn't fair.

GREG: He called us into his office. I told him: "*Voy a
casar con esta chica, Papa.*" It used to piss him off when
I spoke Spanish. So, no, I didn't say it like that. I said,
"I'd like your permission to marry, sir." He just
nodded. Evalina smiled. She'd been so damned loco
scared he'd say no. Then he put his hand on Evalina's
head and took hold of her long braid. *(Beat)* Then gave
her arm a quick twist and she was lying on the floor.
She was so surprised, she couldn't make a noise.

(Lifts his foot and balances. GEORGE *and* DAVID *are now
listening to him.)*

GREG: No. It's not good enough.

(Suddenly grabs DAVID *by the collar and swings him to the
floor)*

GREG: She was so surprised, she couldn't make a noise.

DAVID: *(Protesting)* Hey!

GREG: Shut up.

DAVID: I'm not taking part—

*(*DAVID *breaks off as* GREG *kicks him violently.)*

DAVID: Shut the fuck up! I said: She was so surprised
that she didn't make a noise. *(He lifts his foot.)* And then
he did this.

(Puts his foot on DAVID'*s throat.* DAVID *is passive.*
GREG *speaks as his father.)*

GREG: "This isn't the first time I've had to do this. Don't
worry about it, son, it's just like getting your finger
pricked. Ask your Mother." *(Beat)* And then he brought
his boot heel down, hard, on her abdomen. *(Makes a
sound of air escaping from his lips)* That was the sound
that escaped from Evalina's lips. Can you make that
sound, David? *(Jerks* DAVID *by the hair)* Come on. Try it.

*(*GREG *makes the sound again.* DAVID *is silent. Then* GREG
steps over and away from DAVID*.)*

GREG: Then there was no sound. *Nada. Nada.* I could
feel the warm slide of piss running down my leg into
my shoe. *Cuando Evalina se despierto,* I drove her home.
She was already bleeding it out. *(Beat)* Over breakfast
the next morning he asked me...he asked me....
(He breaks off.)

DAVID: *(Without malice)* He asked you if you'd decided
to postpone the wedding.

GREG: Yeah. *(Beat)* Well, it was a year later. I hadn't
been home in a while. I came by to visit my mother.
Father was out on patrol. We were just talkin' shop
while she was doing the wash. I asked her why she
never had any more kids after me. She just shrugged.
I came right out and told her about me and Evalina,
about almost having to marry, about Father helping
us out. I watched her pour a whole bottle of detergent
in the wash. Then she said, like she might be saying
"That's the third load today", "I thought mine were
the only ones". Then she hit me.

(He moves to DAVID*, takes* DAVID'*s hand, and uses it to
smack himself in the face. Then* DAVID *tunes in on the
role and now* DAVID *plays* GREG'*s Mother, but with no
affectations in his voice.)*

DAVID: And you did nothing? *(Smacks GREG again)*
And you did nothing? *(Smacks GREG again, harder)*
And you did nothing?

GREG: The kid would have been three fourths beaner,
Ma. Not a hundred percent, like you, but three fourths.
Three fourths. An almost. A not quite. A partly.
A fuckin' percentage. And he'd never be able to
grow up and be like his father, Ma. Like I can never
grow up and be like you, no matter how hard I try.
(He moves to GEORGE.) She spit at me.

*(GREG is expecting GEORGE to spit at him. When he doesn't,
GREG pushes him.)*

GREG: *(Louder)* She spit at me. Hey! *(Pushes him)* Hey!

*(GEORGE spits him in the face. GREG turns his story back to
the public.)*

GREG: That's right. *(quietly)* When my father walked
through the door that night, "bang", my mother shot
him in the throat, bull's-eye through the adam's. *(Sings)*
Oh, Evalina, no llores mas por mi
Porque vamanos to the border
Con cervezas cross my knee
So I'm here. The border. It keeps me in line. I mean,
what if I just gave up this huntin'? I might start going
weird.

GEORGE: Quit it, Greg.

GREG: I mean, I might start feeling sorry for Evalina
again, go track her down. Find out where she went to.

DAVID: Enough of this old boy.

GREG: I might even take that gun of his I've got hidden
under a floorboard in my room.

GEORGE: *(Becoming more agitated)* Stop it!

GREG: I might go out hunting. But maybe not for
beaners this time.

GEORGE: I can't listen to you anymore!

GREG: And what if I got even weirder and went after some of you too. I don't know. I mean, you saw him lift his foot over her belly, didn't you? *(Laughs, turns to* DAVID *and* GEORGE *and says calmly)* And you did nothing? *(Turns back to public/border)* And you did nothing? *(Beat)* And you did nothing?

GEORGE: Shut the fuck up!

GREG: I mean, he was the law, your law, and she was just the cheap labor.

*(*GEORGE *punches* GREG *in the face.* GREG *falls down.)*

DAVID: Get the fuck back in the car or this will be the last time we take you shopping.

*(*GREG *gets up as though obeying* DAVID *and goes to the car, but then he snatches the gun.* GREG *raises the gun and aims at them.)*

GEORGE: No, Greg. Put that down.

DAVID: Stay calm, big boy. Take a deep breath.

GREG: *(Speaks calmly and with complete assurance)* Shut up. You're both dead. *(Beat)* Hey, I look good, don't I?

DAVID: Brilliant.

GREG: I've never been more brilliant in all my life. *(Beat)* You're finished. Both of you.

DAVID: Listen, Greggie.

GREG: No. I'm not going to listen. You're going to listen.

GEORGE: Jesus, Greg.

DAVID: You're not playing the game.

GREG: But I am. *(Beat)* Trust me. *(Beat)* Hey, let's play one more time? Which one should we play, David? Once upon a time in the land of radishes?

DAVID: Listen to me a minute. If you'd just—

GREG: *(Interrupts)* No. Not that one. We're tired of that one. So tell me, David, how do you spell relief? *(Beat)* My story is about halves. *(Lifts shirt)* Will you look at this? Split down the middle. But which side is which? I mean, when the moment hit you, when the crisis struck, which did you choose, Hostess or Sara Lee? J V C or Sony? I mean, isn't that the simple beauty of it: Who can afford to hire a maid and who can't afford not to be one?

(GEORGE moves slightly, as though he is thinking to run for it.)

GEORGE: Let me go, Greg. I got to get home.

GREG: Hey, don't you want to play a game? This is your game, David. I say the words and you try and put your mind to work somewhere else so the words won't get to you. Now, think hard about the first time you put your tongue in someone else's mouth, or map it out in your head how you're gonna change things in your neighborhood. Or how about this one: picture how your sister looked when you left her lying there in the park, saying: *(Softly)* No. *(Beat)* David. No. David. No.

(Slaps DAVID in the face, though not hard. DAVID is passive.)

GREG: David. No. *(Beat)* Now, I dare you not to switch out, not to turn off. O K? "I pledge allegiance, to the flag, of the United...." Hold it. Let's start over. Make it harder this time. *(Pokes him with the gun)* Hey. Pay attention. Isn't this what you taught me?

(He puts the gun in DAVID's hand and places the gun at his own forehead. They are both holding it now.)

GREG: Come on, David. Show us your stuff. *(He kneels.)* "I pledge allegiance, to the flag of the United States of—

(Knocks DAVID *so* DAVID *says the rest of the pledge with him.)*

GREG & DAVID: —America. And to the Republic for which it stands, one nation, under God, indivisible, with *(Beat)* liberty and justice for all."

(Stands and takes the gun back from DAVID*)*

GREG: David. No. *(Beat)* The show's over. *(Beat)* O-V-E-R! *(Beat)* George, get out of here.

*(*GEORGE *doesn't move.* GREG *speaks gently.)*

GREG: Hey, now and then, you were funny. I mean it. *(Beat)* So go home, Camel-boy. *(To* DAVID*)* But I can't let you off that easy, David. Yeah, I like you. But I'm your nightmare now, your very own one-hundred-percent All American, pure beef Wetback, and I'm gonna stay right here, light up this border, *(Beat)* but how about from the other side this time. *(Beat) Y de ahora en adelante ya no voy a hablar mas el ingles. Yo necesito mis proprias palabras para..para...luchar. Si, ya se que has escuchado todo eso antes, pero esto vez...*Watch out!

(Pushes DAVID *to kneel.* DAVID *does not resist.* GREG *pulls* DAVID'*s head back by the hair and kisses him violently on the forehead.)*

GREG: Listen. Something just had to give. It's nothing personal. *(Raises gun to* DAVID'*s temple.* GREG *speaks calmly and slowly.)* We were always friends.

(There are some moments of silence as we wait for the shot. Nothing happens.)

GREG: *Escucha*, David. With all that *inteligente* you bought— *(Holds the gun up in front of* DAVID'*s face)* —can you read this? Right here? Can you read it? It doesn't say Taiwan or Japan this time. On the barrel, you can read it if you squint. You see what it says? *(He steps back from the two of them.)* It says: Made in the U S A. *(Beat)*

Here. *(Holds out gun to* DAVID *and* GEORGE*)* You can
have it back.

(Neither GEORGE *nor* DAVID *moves.* GREG *drops the gun at
their feet. He begins to exit. Lights black out just as he leaves
the stage.)*

END OF PLAY